50 Healthy Salad Recipes for Home

By: Kelly Johnson

Table of Contents

- Kale and Quinoa Salad
- Spinach and Strawberry Salad
- Mediterranean Chickpea Salad
- Avocado and Black Bean Salad
- Grilled Vegetable Salad
- Greek Salad with Tofu
- Roasted Beet and Goat Cheese Salad
- Sweet Potato and Arugula Salad
- Thai Peanut Salad
- Broccoli and Cauliflower Salad
- Apple and Walnut Salad
- Cucumber and Tomato Salad
- Lentil and Feta Salad
- Zucchini Noodle Salad
- Mixed Berry Salad
- Carrot and Raisin Salad
- Asian Cabbage Salad
- Citrus Avocado Salad
- Warm Farro Salad
- Watermelon and Feta Salad
- Quinoa and Black Bean Salad
- Chickpea and Cucumber Salad
- Spinach and Avocado Salad
- Roasted Brussels Sprout Salad
- Asian Noodle Salad
- Corn and Tomato Salad
- Mixed Green Salad with Nuts
- Sweet Corn and Avocado Salad
- Edamame and Carrot Salad
- Roasted Butternut Squash Salad
- Cabbage and Apple Slaw
- Pomegranate and Kale Salad

- Red Bean and Quinoa Salad
- Roasted Red Pepper Salad
- Pear and Gorgonzola Salad
- Fennel and Orange Salad
- Grilled Peach Salad
- Spinach and Mushroom Salad
- Chickpea and Red Pepper Salad
- Avocado and Citrus Salad
- Mediterranean Couscous Salad
- Herb and Tomato Salad
- Roasted Cauliflower Salad
- Green Bean and Almond Salad
- Sweet Potato and Kale Salad
- Brussels Sprout and Bacon Salad
- Avocado and Black Bean Quinoa Salad
- Beet and Orange Salad
- Cranberry and Spinach Salad
- Lentil and Sweet Potato Salad

Kale and Quinoa Salad

Ingredients:

- **For the Salad:**
    - 1 cup quinoa
    - 2 cups water or vegetable broth
    - 4 cups kale, stems removed and chopped
    - 1 cup cherry tomatoes, halved
    - 1/2 cucumber, diced
    - 1/4 cup red onion, finely chopped
    - 1/4 cup crumbled feta cheese (or vegan feta)
    - 1/4 cup sliced almonds or walnuts
    - 1/4 cup dried cranberries or raisins
    - 1 avocado, diced (optional)
- **For the Dressing:**
    - 3 tbsp extra-virgin olive oil
    - 2 tbsp lemon juice (about 1 lemon)
    - 1 tbsp Dijon mustard
    - 1 tbsp honey or maple syrup (for a vegan option)
    - 1 clove garlic, minced
    - Salt and black pepper to taste

Instructions:

1. **Cook the Quinoa:**
    - Rinse quinoa under cold water.
    - In a medium saucepan, bring water or vegetable broth to a boil.
    - Add quinoa, reduce heat, cover, and simmer for 15 minutes or until the liquid is absorbed and quinoa is tender. Fluff with a fork and let cool.
2. **Prepare the Kale:**
    - In a large bowl, massage the chopped kale with a bit of olive oil and a pinch of salt until the leaves are tender.
3. **Combine the Salad:**
    - Add the cooked quinoa, cherry tomatoes, cucumber, red onion, feta cheese, almonds or walnuts, dried cranberries, and avocado (if using) to the bowl with kale.
4. **Make the Dressing:**
    - In a small bowl or jar, whisk together olive oil, lemon juice, Dijon mustard, honey or maple syrup, minced garlic, salt, and black pepper.
5. **Toss and Serve:**
    - Drizzle the dressing over the salad and toss to combine.

6. **Serve:**
   - Enjoy immediately or refrigerate for later. The flavors develop more after a few hours.

Tips:

- **For Extra Flavor:** Add a sprinkle of nutritional yeast or a pinch of red pepper flakes.
- **For a Protein Boost:** Top with grilled chicken or tofu.

This Kale and Quinoa Salad is vibrant, protein-packed, and perfect for a healthy meal!

Spinach and Strawberry Salad

Ingredients:

- **For the Salad:**
    - 4 cups fresh spinach, washed and dried
    - 1 cup strawberries, hulled and sliced
    - 1/4 cup red onion, thinly sliced
    - 1/4 cup crumbled feta cheese (or goat cheese)
    - 1/4 cup sliced almonds or pecans
    - 1/4 cup dried cranberries or raisins
- **For the Dressing:**
    - 3 tbsp extra-virgin olive oil
    - 2 tbsp balsamic vinegar
    - 1 tbsp honey or maple syrup
    - 1 tsp Dijon mustard
    - Salt and black pepper to taste

Instructions:

1. **Prepare the Salad:**
    - In a large bowl, combine the spinach, sliced strawberries, red onion, crumbled feta cheese, almonds or pecans, and dried cranberries.
2. **Make the Dressing:**
    - In a small bowl or jar, whisk together olive oil, balsamic vinegar, honey or maple syrup, Dijon mustard, salt, and black pepper until well combined.
3. **Toss and Serve:**
    - Drizzle the dressing over the salad and toss gently to combine.
4. **Serve:**
    - Serve immediately for the freshest taste.

Tips:

- For Extra Flavor: Add a sprinkle of chia seeds or poppy seeds to the salad.
- For a Heartier Salad: Top with grilled chicken or tofu.

Enjoy this Spinach and Strawberry Salad as a light, sweet, and savory meal!

Mediterranean Chickpea Salad

Ingredients:

- **For the Salad:**
    - 1 can (15 oz) chickpeas, drained and rinsed
    - 1 cup cherry tomatoes, halved
    - 1 cucumber, diced
    - 1/4 cup red onion, finely chopped
    - 1/2 cup Kalamata olives, pitted and sliced
    - 1/4 cup crumbled feta cheese (or vegan feta)
    - 1/4 cup fresh parsley, chopped
    - 1/4 cup fresh mint, chopped (optional)
- **For the Dressing:**
    - 3 tbsp extra-virgin olive oil
    - 2 tbsp red wine vinegar or lemon juice
    - 1 clove garlic, minced
    - 1 tsp dried oregano
    - 1/2 tsp dried basil
    - Salt and black pepper to taste

Instructions:

1. **Prepare the Salad:**
    - In a large bowl, combine the chickpeas, cherry tomatoes, cucumber, red onion, olives, feta cheese, parsley, and mint (if using).
2. **Make the Dressing:**
    - In a small bowl or jar, whisk together olive oil, red wine vinegar or lemon juice, minced garlic, oregano, basil, salt, and black pepper.
3. **Toss and Serve:**
    - Pour the dressing over the salad and toss gently to combine.
4. **Serve:**
    - Serve immediately or refrigerate for later. The flavors meld nicely after a few hours.

Tips:

- **For Extra Flavor:** Add a pinch of red pepper flakes or a splash of hot sauce.
- **For Added Crunch:** Toss in some chopped bell peppers or sliced radishes.

This Mediterranean Chickpea Salad is both refreshing and satisfying, perfect for a healthy lunch or side dish!

Avocado and Black Bean Salad

Ingredients:

- **For the Salad:**
    - 1 can (15 oz) black beans, drained and rinsed
    - 1 large avocado, diced
    - 1 cup cherry tomatoes, halved
    - 1/2 cup red onion, finely chopped
    - 1/2 cup corn kernels (fresh, frozen, or canned)
    - 1/4 cup fresh cilantro, chopped
    - 1 jalapeño, seeded and finely chopped (optional, for heat)
    - 1 lime, juiced
    - Salt and black pepper to taste
- **For the Dressing:**
    - 3 tbsp extra-virgin olive oil
    - 1 tbsp lime juice
    - 1 clove garlic, minced
    - 1/2 tsp cumin
    - 1/2 tsp paprika
    - Salt and black pepper to taste

Instructions:

1. **Prepare the Salad:**
    - In a large bowl, combine the black beans, diced avocado, cherry tomatoes, red onion, corn, cilantro, and jalapeño (if using).
2. **Make the Dressing:**
    - In a small bowl or jar, whisk together olive oil, lime juice, minced garlic, cumin, paprika, salt, and black pepper.
3. **Toss and Serve:**
    - Drizzle the dressing over the salad and gently toss to combine.
4. **Serve:**
    - Serve immediately or refrigerate for up to a few hours. The salad is best enjoyed fresh.

Tips:

- **For Extra Flavor:** Add a sprinkle of crumbled feta cheese or avocado slices.
- **For a Protein Boost:** Top with grilled chicken or shrimp.

This Avocado and Black Bean Salad is vibrant, satisfying, and packed with flavors and nutrients!

Grilled Vegetable Salad

Ingredients:

- **For the Salad:**
    - 1 red bell pepper, sliced
    - 1 yellow bell pepper, sliced
    - 1 zucchini, sliced
    - 1 red onion, sliced
    - 1 cup cherry tomatoes
    - 1 cup asparagus spears, trimmed
    - 2 tbsp olive oil
    - Salt and black pepper to taste
    - 1/4 cup fresh basil, chopped (optional)
- **For the Dressing:**
    - 3 tbsp balsamic vinegar
    - 2 tbsp extra-virgin olive oil
    - 1 tsp Dijon mustard
    - 1 clove garlic, minced
    - 1 tsp dried oregano
    - Salt and black pepper to taste

Instructions:

1. **Prepare the Vegetables:**
    - Preheat your grill or grill pan over medium-high heat.
    - Toss the bell peppers, zucchini, red onion, cherry tomatoes, and asparagus with olive oil, salt, and black pepper.
2. **Grill the Vegetables:**
    - Grill the vegetables in batches if necessary. Place them on the grill and cook, turning occasionally, until they are tender and have grill marks, about 3-5 minutes per side for the peppers and zucchini, and 2-3 minutes per side for the asparagus.
    - Remove the vegetables from the grill and let them cool slightly. Cut them into bite-sized pieces if needed.
3. **Make the Dressing:**
    - In a small bowl or jar, whisk together balsamic vinegar, olive oil, Dijon mustard, minced garlic, dried oregano, salt, and black pepper.
4. **Combine the Salad:**
    - In a large bowl, combine the grilled vegetables and drizzle with the dressing.
    - Toss gently to coat the vegetables with the dressing.
5. **Garnish and Serve:**

- Garnish with chopped fresh basil if desired.
- Serve warm or at room temperature.

Tips:

- **For Added Flavor:** Sprinkle with crumbled feta cheese or shaved Parmesan before serving.
- **For Extra Texture:** Add toasted pine nuts or sunflower seeds.
- **For a Complete Meal:** Top with quinoa or grilled chicken.

Enjoy this Grilled Vegetable Salad as a vibrant and healthy option for a meal or as a flavorful side dish!

Greek Salad with Tofu

Ingredients:

- **For the Salad:**
    - 1 block (14 oz) firm tofu, drained and pressed
    - 4 cups mixed greens or chopped romaine lettuce
    - 1 cup cherry tomatoes, halved
    - 1 cucumber, diced
    - 1/4 cup red onion, thinly sliced
    - 1/2 cup Kalamata olives, pitted
    - 1/2 cup crumbled feta cheese (or vegan feta)
    - 1/4 cup fresh parsley, chopped
    - 1/4 cup fresh mint, chopped (optional)
- **For the Dressing:**
    - 3 tbsp extra-virgin olive oil
    - 2 tbsp red wine vinegar
    - 1 tsp dried oregano
    - 1 clove garlic, minced
    - 1 tsp Dijon mustard
    - Salt and black pepper to taste
- **For the Tofu:**
    - 2 tbsp olive oil
    - 1 tbsp soy sauce or tamari
    - 1 tsp dried oregano
    - 1/2 tsp garlic powder
    - Salt and black pepper to taste

Instructions:

1. **Prepare the Tofu:**
    - Cut the tofu into bite-sized cubes.
    - In a bowl, mix together olive oil, soy sauce or tamari, dried oregano, garlic powder, salt, and black pepper.
    - Toss the tofu cubes in the marinade and let sit for 10-15 minutes.
    - Heat a skillet over medium heat and cook the tofu cubes, turning occasionally, until they are golden and crispy on all sides, about 8-10 minutes. Remove from heat and let cool slightly.
2. **Prepare the Salad:**
    - In a large bowl, combine the mixed greens, cherry tomatoes, cucumber, red onion, Kalamata olives, and crumbled feta cheese.
    - Add the cooked tofu to the salad.

3. **Make the Dressing:**
   - In a small bowl or jar, whisk together olive oil, red wine vinegar, dried oregano, minced garlic, Dijon mustard, salt, and black pepper.
4. **Combine the Salad:**
   - Drizzle the dressing over the salad and toss gently to combine.
   - Garnish with chopped parsley and mint if desired.
5. **Serve:**
   - Serve immediately for the freshest taste, or refrigerate for later.

Tips:

- **For Extra Flavor:** Add a splash of lemon juice or a sprinkle of red pepper flakes.
- **For a Heartier Meal:** Serve the salad with pita bread or alongside quinoa or couscous.

This Greek Salad with Tofu is a vibrant, protein-packed dish that's perfect for lunch or a light dinner!

Roasted Beet and Goat Cheese Salad

Ingredients:

- **For the Salad:**
    - 4 medium beets, peeled and cut into wedges
    - 2 tbsp olive oil
    - Salt and black pepper to taste
    - 4 cups mixed salad greens (e.g., arugula, spinach, or baby greens)
    - 1/4 cup crumbled goat cheese
    - 1/4 cup walnuts, toasted (or pecans)
    - 1/4 cup dried cranberries or pomegranate seeds (optional)
    - 1/4 red onion, thinly sliced
- **For the Dressing:**
    - 3 tbsp extra-virgin olive oil
    - 2 tbsp balsamic vinegar
    - 1 tsp Dijon mustard
    - 1 tbsp honey or maple syrup (for a vegan option)
    - 1 clove garlic, minced
    - Salt and black pepper to taste

Instructions:

1. **Roast the Beets:**
    - Preheat your oven to 400°F (200°C).
    - Toss the beet wedges with olive oil, salt, and black pepper. Spread them out in a single layer on a baking sheet.
    - Roast the beets in the preheated oven for 30-35 minutes, or until tender and slightly caramelized, turning once halfway through. Allow them to cool slightly.
2. **Prepare the Salad:**
    - In a large bowl, combine the mixed salad greens, crumbled goat cheese, toasted walnuts, dried cranberries or pomegranate seeds (if using), and sliced red onion.
3. **Make the Dressing:**
    - In a small bowl or jar, whisk together olive oil, balsamic vinegar, Dijon mustard, honey or maple syrup, minced garlic, salt, and black pepper.
4. **Combine the Salad:**
    - Add the roasted beets to the salad.
    - Drizzle with the dressing and toss gently to combine.
5. **Serve:**
    - Serve immediately or refrigerate for a short time. The salad is best enjoyed fresh.

Tips:

- **For Extra Crunch:** Add some thinly sliced radishes or additional toasted nuts.
- **For a Heartier Meal:** Top with grilled chicken or chickpeas.

This Roasted Beet and Goat Cheese Salad offers a delightful mix of flavors and textures, perfect for a satisfying lunch or as a side dish!

Sweet Potato and Arugula Salad

Ingredients:

- **For the Salad:**
    - 2 large sweet potatoes, peeled and cubed
    - 2 tbsp olive oil
    - Salt and black pepper to taste
    - 4 cups arugula
    - 1/4 cup crumbled feta cheese (or goat cheese)
    - 1/4 cup toasted pecans or walnuts
    - 1/4 cup dried cranberries or pomegranate seeds
    - 1 small red onion, thinly sliced
- **For the Dressing:**
    - 3 tbsp extra-virgin olive oil
    - 2 tbsp balsamic vinegar
    - 1 tbsp maple syrup or honey
    - 1 tsp Dijon mustard
    - 1 clove garlic, minced
    - Salt and black pepper to taste

Instructions:

1. **Roast the Sweet Potatoes:**
    - Preheat your oven to 400°F (200°C).
    - Toss the sweet potato cubes with olive oil, salt, and black pepper.
    - Spread them out in a single layer on a baking sheet.
    - Roast in the preheated oven for 25-30 minutes, or until tender and slightly caramelized, turning once halfway through. Allow to cool slightly.
2. **Prepare the Salad:**
    - In a large bowl, combine the arugula, crumbled feta cheese, toasted pecans or walnuts, dried cranberries or pomegranate seeds, and sliced red onion.
3. **Make the Dressing:**
    - In a small bowl or jar, whisk together olive oil, balsamic vinegar, maple syrup or honey, Dijon mustard, minced garlic, salt, and black pepper.
4. **Combine the Salad:**
    - Add the roasted sweet potatoes to the salad.
    - Drizzle with the dressing and toss gently to combine.
5. **Serve:**
    - Serve immediately or refrigerate for a short time. The salad is best enjoyed fresh.

Tips:

- **For Extra Flavor:** Add a sprinkle of pumpkin seeds or a few fresh herbs like basil or cilantro.
- **For a Heartier Salad:** Top with grilled chicken or tofu for added protein.

This Sweet Potato and Arugula Salad is a delicious mix of flavors and textures, making it a perfect choice for a healthy lunch or as a side dish for dinner!

Thai Peanut Salad

Ingredients:

- **For the Salad:**
    - 4 cups shredded cabbage (green or purple, or a mix)
    - 1 cup shredded carrots
    - 1 cup snap peas or snow peas, trimmed and halved
    - 1/2 red bell pepper, thinly sliced
    - 1/2 cup fresh cilantro, chopped
    - 1/4 cup chopped green onions
    - 1/4 cup roasted peanuts, chopped (for garnish)
    - 1/2 cup edamame (optional, for added protein)
- **For the Thai Peanut Dressing:**
    - 1/4 cup creamy peanut butter
    - 2 tbsp soy sauce or tamari
    - 2 tbsp rice vinegar
    - 1 tbsp honey or maple syrup (for a vegan option)
    - 1 tbsp lime juice
    - 1 clove garlic, minced
    - 1 tsp grated fresh ginger (or 1/2 tsp ground ginger)
    - 1-2 tbsp water (to thin the dressing as needed)
    - 1/2 tsp sriracha or red pepper flakes (optional, for heat)

Instructions:

1. **Prepare the Salad Ingredients:**
    - In a large bowl, combine shredded cabbage, shredded carrots, snap peas, red bell pepper, cilantro, and green onions.
2. **Make the Thai Peanut Dressing:**
    - In a small bowl or jar, whisk together peanut butter, soy sauce or tamari, rice vinegar, honey or maple syrup, lime juice, minced garlic, grated ginger, and sriracha or red pepper flakes if using.
    - Add water a tablespoon at a time until the dressing reaches your desired consistency (it should be smooth and pourable).
3. **Combine the Salad:**
    - Pour the dressing over the salad and toss gently to coat all the vegetables evenly.
    - If using, fold in the edamame.
4. **Garnish and Serve:**
    - Garnish with chopped roasted peanuts before serving.

Tips:

- **For Extra Crunch:** Add a handful of toasted sesame seeds or crispy rice noodles.
- **For Additional Protein:** Top with grilled chicken, tofu, or shrimp.

This Thai Peanut Salad is a deliciously crunchy and tangy dish that's perfect for a healthy lunch or a refreshing side!

Broccoli and Cauliflower Salad

Ingredients:

- **For the Salad:**
    - 2 cups broccoli florets
    - 2 cups cauliflower florets
    - 1/4 cup red onion, finely chopped
    - 1/4 cup shredded carrots
    - 1/4 cup sunflower seeds or chopped nuts (e.g., almonds or walnuts)
    - 1/4 cup dried cranberries or raisins
    - 1/4 cup shredded cheese (e.g., cheddar or Parmesan) (optional)
- **For the Dressing:**
    - 1/2 cup Greek yogurt or mayonnaise
    - 2 tbsp apple cider vinegar or white wine vinegar
    - 1 tbsp honey or maple syrup (for a vegan option)
    - 1 tsp Dijon mustard
    - Salt and black pepper to taste

Instructions:

1. **Prepare the Vegetables:**
    - Steam or blanch the broccoli and cauliflower florets until they are just tender but still crisp, about 3-4 minutes. Drain and cool completely. Alternatively, you can use raw florets for a crunchier texture.
2. **Combine the Salad Ingredients:**
    - In a large bowl, mix together the broccoli, cauliflower, red onion, shredded carrots, sunflower seeds, dried cranberries, and shredded cheese if using.
3. **Make the Dressing:**
    - In a small bowl, whisk together Greek yogurt or mayonnaise, apple cider vinegar or white wine vinegar, honey or maple syrup, Dijon mustard, salt, and black pepper.
4. **Combine the Salad:**
    - Pour the dressing over the salad and toss gently to coat all ingredients evenly.
5. **Serve:**
    - Serve immediately or refrigerate for up to a few hours. The flavors develop more after sitting for a while.

Tips:

- **For Extra Flavor:** Add a sprinkle of garlic powder or a few fresh herbs like dill or parsley.
- **For Added Crunch:** Include some crispy bacon bits or croutons.

This Broccoli and Cauliflower Salad is a nutritious and satisfying dish that works well as a side or a light meal!

Apple and Walnut Salad

Ingredients:

- **For the Salad:**
    - 4 cups mixed greens (e.g., spinach, arugula, or baby greens)
    - 1 large apple, cored and thinly sliced (e.g., Granny Smith or Honeycrisp)
    - 1/4 cup walnuts, toasted
    - 1/4 cup crumbled feta cheese (or goat cheese)
    - 1/4 cup dried cranberries or raisins
    - 1/4 red onion, thinly sliced
    - 1/4 cup chopped fresh parsley (optional)
- **For the Dressing:**
    - 3 tbsp extra-virgin olive oil
    - 2 tbsp apple cider vinegar
    - 1 tbsp honey or maple syrup
    - 1 tsp Dijon mustard
    - 1 clove garlic, minced
    - Salt and black pepper to taste

Instructions:

1. **Prepare the Salad:**
    - In a large bowl, combine the mixed greens, apple slices, toasted walnuts, crumbled feta cheese, dried cranberries, and red onion.
2. **Make the Dressing:**
    - In a small bowl or jar, whisk together olive oil, apple cider vinegar, honey or maple syrup, Dijon mustard, minced garlic, salt, and black pepper.
3. **Combine the Salad:**
    - Drizzle the dressing over the salad and toss gently to coat all ingredients evenly.
4. **Garnish and Serve:**
    - Garnish with chopped fresh parsley if desired.
5. **Serve:**
    - Serve immediately for the freshest taste or refrigerate for up to an hour before serving.

Tips:

- **For Extra Crunch:** Add some sliced almonds or croutons.
- **For Additional Flavor:** Include a sprinkle of cinnamon or a few fresh mint leaves.

This Apple and Walnut Salad is a delightful mix of sweet, tangy, and crunchy elements, perfect for a refreshing lunch or as a side dish!

Cucumber and Tomato Salad

Ingredients:

- **For the Salad:**
    - 2 large cucumbers, peeled and sliced
    - 1 cup cherry tomatoes, halved
    - 1/4 red onion, thinly sliced
    - 1/4 cup fresh basil or parsley, chopped
    - 1/4 cup feta cheese, crumbled (optional)
- **For the Dressing:**
    - 3 tbsp extra-virgin olive oil
    - 2 tbsp red wine vinegar or lemon juice
    - 1 tsp Dijon mustard
    - 1 clove garlic, minced
    - 1/2 tsp dried oregano
    - Salt and black pepper to taste

Instructions:

1. **Prepare the Salad:**
    - In a large bowl, combine the sliced cucumbers, cherry tomatoes, red onion, and fresh basil or parsley.
2. **Make the Dressing:**
    - In a small bowl or jar, whisk together olive oil, red wine vinegar or lemon juice, Dijon mustard, minced garlic, dried oregano, salt, and black pepper.
3. **Combine the Salad:**
    - Drizzle the dressing over the salad and toss gently to coat all ingredients evenly.
4. **Garnish and Serve:**
    - If using, sprinkle crumbled feta cheese over the salad.
5. **Serve:**
    - Serve immediately for the freshest taste, or chill for up to an hour before serving.

Tips:

- **For Extra Crunch:** Add sliced bell peppers or radishes.
- **For a Heartier Salad:** Include some cooked quinoa or chickpeas.

This Cucumber and Tomato Salad is light, refreshing, and perfect for a quick side or a light lunch!

Lentil and Feta Salad

Ingredients:

- **For the Salad:**
    - 1 cup dried green or brown lentils (or 2 1/2 cups cooked lentils)
    - 1 cup cherry tomatoes, halved
    - 1/2 cucumber, diced
    - 1/4 cup red onion, finely chopped
    - 1/4 cup fresh parsley, chopped
    - 1/4 cup crumbled feta cheese
    - 1/4 cup kalamata olives, pitted and sliced (optional)
- **For the Dressing:**
    - 3 tbsp extra-virgin olive oil
    - 2 tbsp red wine vinegar or lemon juice
    - 1 tsp Dijon mustard
    - 1 clove garlic, minced
    - 1/2 tsp dried oregano
    - Salt and black pepper to taste

Instructions:

1. **Cook the Lentils:**
    - Rinse the lentils under cold water.
    - In a pot, cover the lentils with water (about 2-3 cups) and bring to a boil.
    - Reduce heat to low and simmer for 20-25 minutes, or until lentils are tender but still firm. Avoid overcooking. Drain and let cool.
2. **Prepare the Salad:**
    - In a large bowl, combine the cooked lentils, cherry tomatoes, cucumber, red onion, parsley, and crumbled feta cheese.
    - Add the kalamata olives if using.
3. **Make the Dressing:**
    - In a small bowl or jar, whisk together olive oil, red wine vinegar or lemon juice, Dijon mustard, minced garlic, dried oregano, salt, and black pepper.
4. **Combine the Salad:**
    - Pour the dressing over the salad and toss gently to combine.
5. **Serve:**
    - Serve immediately or chill for about 30 minutes to allow the flavors to meld.

Tips:

- **For Extra Flavor:** Add a pinch of cumin or a sprinkle of red pepper flakes for some heat.

- **For Added Texture:** Toss in some chopped nuts or seeds, like almonds or pumpkin seeds.

This Lentil and Feta Salad is hearty, flavorful, and makes a great meal on its own or as a side dish!

Zucchini Noodle Salad

Ingredients:

- **For the Salad:**
    - 4 medium zucchinis, spiralized or julienned into noodles
    - 1 cup cherry tomatoes, halved
    - 1/2 cup sliced bell peppers (any color)
    - 1/4 cup red onion, thinly sliced
    - 1/4 cup fresh basil or parsley, chopped
    - 1/4 cup crumbled feta cheese (optional)
- **For the Dressing:**
    - 3 tbsp extra-virgin olive oil
    - 2 tbsp lemon juice
    - 1 tbsp red wine vinegar
    - 1 tsp Dijon mustard
    - 1 clove garlic, minced
    - 1/2 tsp dried oregano
    - Salt and black pepper to taste

Instructions:

1. **Prepare the Zucchini Noodles:**
    - If using fresh zucchini, spiralize or julienne them into noodles. Lightly salt the zucchini noodles and let them sit for about 10 minutes to release excess moisture. Pat dry with paper towels.
2. **Prepare the Salad:**
    - In a large bowl, combine the zucchini noodles, cherry tomatoes, bell peppers, red onion, and fresh basil or parsley.
    - Add crumbled feta cheese if desired.
3. **Make the Dressing:**
    - In a small bowl or jar, whisk together olive oil, lemon juice, red wine vinegar, Dijon mustard, minced garlic, dried oregano, salt, and black pepper.
4. **Combine the Salad:**
    - Drizzle the dressing over the salad and toss gently to coat all ingredients evenly.
5. **Serve:**
    - Serve immediately for the freshest taste, or chill for a short time if you prefer.

Tips:

- **For Extra Crunch:** Add some sliced almonds or sunflower seeds.
- **For a Protein Boost:** Top with grilled chicken or tofu.

This Zucchini Noodle Salad is a refreshing and light dish, perfect for a healthy lunch or as a side dish!

Mixed Berry Salad

Ingredients:

- **For the Salad:**
    - 1 cup strawberries, hulled and sliced
    - 1 cup blueberries
    - 1 cup raspberries
    - 1/2 cup blackberries
    - 1 cup mixed greens (e.g., baby spinach, arugula, or lettuce)
    - 1/4 cup crumbled feta cheese or goat cheese (optional)
    - 1/4 cup chopped fresh mint or basil (optional)
    - 1/4 cup toasted nuts or seeds (e.g., almonds, walnuts, or sunflower seeds) (optional)
- **For the Dressing:**
    - 3 tbsp honey or maple syrup
    - 2 tbsp lemon juice
    - 1 tbsp extra-virgin olive oil
    - 1/2 tsp vanilla extract (optional)
    - Pinch of salt

Instructions:

1. **Prepare the Berries:**
    - Wash and gently pat dry all the berries. Slice the strawberries if they are large.
2. **Prepare the Salad:**
    - In a large bowl, combine the mixed greens, strawberries, blueberries, raspberries, and blackberries.
    - Add crumbled feta cheese or goat cheese and fresh mint or basil if using.
    - Sprinkle with toasted nuts or seeds for extra texture if desired.
3. **Make the Dressing:**
    - In a small bowl or jar, whisk together honey or maple syrup, lemon juice, olive oil, vanilla extract (if using), and a pinch of salt.
4. **Combine the Salad:**
    - Drizzle the dressing over the salad and toss gently to coat all the ingredients.
5. **Serve:**
    - Serve immediately for the freshest taste, or refrigerate for a short time before serving.

Tips:

- **For Extra Flavor:** Add a sprinkle of chia seeds or flaxseeds.

- **For a Heartier Salad:** Include some quinoa or granola for added substance.

This Mixed Berry Salad is a delightful combination of sweet and tangy flavors, making it a perfect choice for a light lunch, brunch, or as a refreshing side dish!

Carrot and Raisin Salad

Ingredients:

- **For the Salad:**
    - 4 cups shredded carrots (about 4-5 large carrots)
    - 1/2 cup raisins
    - 1/4 cup chopped walnuts or pecans (optional)
    - 1/4 cup chopped fresh parsley or cilantro (optional)
- **For the Dressing:**
    - 1/2 cup Greek yogurt or mayonnaise
    - 2 tbsp honey or maple syrup
    - 1 tbsp apple cider vinegar or lemon juice
    - 1 tsp Dijon mustard (optional)
    - Salt and black pepper to taste

Instructions:

1. **Prepare the Carrots:**
    - Peel and shred the carrots using a box grater or a food processor. Place them in a large bowl.
2. **Prepare the Salad Ingredients:**
    - Add the raisins to the bowl with the shredded carrots.
    - If using, add the chopped walnuts or pecans and fresh parsley or cilantro.
3. **Make the Dressing:**
    - In a small bowl, whisk together Greek yogurt or mayonnaise, honey or maple syrup, apple cider vinegar or lemon juice, Dijon mustard (if using), salt, and black pepper.
4. **Combine the Salad:**
    - Pour the dressing over the carrot and raisin mixture.
    - Toss everything together until well coated with the dressing.
5. **Serve:**
    - Serve immediately, or refrigerate for at least 30 minutes to let the flavors meld.

Tips:

- **For Extra Crunch:** Add some sliced apples or celery.
- **For a Creamier Texture:** Use extra Greek yogurt or mayonnaise as needed.
- **For a Light Version:** Use low-fat Greek yogurt or a vegan mayo alternative.

This Carrot and Raisin Salad is a sweet and crunchy side dish that's perfect for a healthy lunch or as a complement to any meal!

Asian Cabbage Salad

Ingredients:

- **For the Salad:**
    - 4 cups shredded green cabbage
    - 2 cups shredded red cabbage
    - 1 cup shredded carrots
    - 1 cup snap peas, thinly sliced (or use snow peas)
    - 1/2 cup sliced bell peppers (any color)
    - 1/4 cup chopped green onions
    - 1/4 cup chopped fresh cilantro
    - 1/4 cup toasted sesame seeds
    - 1/4 cup chopped peanuts or cashews (optional)
- **For the Dressing:**
    - 1/4 cup soy sauce or tamari
    - 2 tbsp rice vinegar
    - 1 tbsp sesame oil
    - 1 tbsp honey or maple syrup
    - 1 tsp freshly grated ginger
    - 1 clove garlic, minced
    - 1 tsp Sriracha or red pepper flakes (optional, for heat)

Instructions:

1. **Prepare the Salad Ingredients:**
    - In a large bowl, combine shredded green cabbage, shredded red cabbage, shredded carrots, snap peas, sliced bell peppers, green onions, and chopped cilantro.
2. **Make the Dressing:**
    - In a small bowl or jar, whisk together soy sauce or tamari, rice vinegar, sesame oil, honey or maple syrup, grated ginger, minced garlic, and Sriracha or red pepper flakes if using.
3. **Combine the Salad:**
    - Pour the dressing over the salad and toss gently to coat all ingredients evenly.
4. **Add Toppings:**
    - Sprinkle with toasted sesame seeds and chopped peanuts or cashews, if desired.
5. **Serve:**
    - Serve immediately, or refrigerate for up to an hour to let the flavors meld.

Tips:

- **For Extra Crunch:** Add some crispy wonton strips or edamame.
- **For a Heartier Salad:** Include some cooked chicken or tofu for added protein.

This Asian Cabbage Salad is a crunchy, flavorful dish that's perfect for a refreshing lunch or as a side dish for dinner!

Citrus Avocado Salad

Ingredients:

- **For the Salad:**
    - 2 large avocados, peeled, pitted, and sliced
    - 1 grapefruit, segmented
    - 1 orange, segmented
    - 1/4 cup thinly sliced red onion
    - 1/4 cup chopped fresh cilantro or basil
    - 1/4 cup crumbled feta cheese or goat cheese (optional)
    - 1/4 cup chopped nuts or seeds (e.g., almonds, pistachios) (optional)
- **For the Dressing:**
    - 3 tbsp extra-virgin olive oil
    - 2 tbsp fresh lime juice
    - 1 tbsp honey or maple syrup
    - 1 tsp Dijon mustard
    - Salt and black pepper to taste

Instructions:

1. **Prepare the Citrus:**
    - Using a sharp knife, peel and segment the grapefruit and orange. Remove any seeds and set the segments aside.
2. **Prepare the Salad Ingredients:**
    - In a large bowl, gently combine sliced avocados, citrus segments, and thinly sliced red onion.
    - Add chopped cilantro or basil and crumbled feta cheese if using.
3. **Make the Dressing:**
    - In a small bowl or jar, whisk together olive oil, lime juice, honey or maple syrup, Dijon mustard, salt, and black pepper.
4. **Combine the Salad:**
    - Drizzle the dressing over the salad and toss gently to coat the ingredients without mashing the avocados.
5. **Add Toppings:**
    - Sprinkle with chopped nuts or seeds if desired.
6. **Serve:**
    - Serve immediately for the freshest taste.

Tips:

- **For Extra Flavor:** Add a few slices of thinly sliced radish or a sprinkle of chili flakes for a bit of heat.
- **For Added Texture:** Include some mixed greens or a handful of baby spinach.

This Citrus Avocado Salad is a delightful mix of creamy and tangy flavors, perfect for a light lunch or as a bright side dish!

Warm Farro Salad

Ingredients:

- **For the Salad:**
    - 1 cup farro (preferably pearled or semi-pearled)
    - 2 cups water or vegetable broth (for cooking the farro)
    - 1 cup cherry tomatoes, halved
    - 1 cup diced cucumber
    - 1/2 cup red onion, finely chopped
    - 1/2 cup crumbled feta cheese (optional)
    - 1/4 cup kalamata olives, pitted and sliced (optional)
    - 1/4 cup fresh parsley or basil, chopped
- **For the Dressing:**
    - 3 tbsp extra-virgin olive oil
    - 2 tbsp red wine vinegar or lemon juice
    - 1 tbsp Dijon mustard
    - 1 clove garlic, minced
    - 1/2 tsp dried oregano or thyme
    - Salt and black pepper to taste

Instructions:

1. **Cook the Farro:**
    - Rinse the farro under cold water.
    - In a medium pot, bring 2 cups of water or vegetable broth to a boil. Add the farro and reduce the heat to low. Cover and simmer for 20-30 minutes, or until the farro is tender but still chewy. Drain any excess liquid if necessary, and let the farro cool slightly.
2. **Prepare the Salad Ingredients:**
    - In a large bowl, combine the cooked farro, cherry tomatoes, diced cucumber, and red onion.
    - Add crumbled feta cheese and sliced kalamata olives if using.
    - Toss in the chopped fresh parsley or basil.
3. **Make the Dressing:**
    - In a small bowl or jar, whisk together olive oil, red wine vinegar or lemon juice, Dijon mustard, minced garlic, dried oregano or thyme, salt, and black pepper.
4. **Combine the Salad:**
    - Drizzle the dressing over the farro mixture and toss gently to combine.
5. **Serve:**
    - Serve the salad warm or at room temperature.

Tips:

- **For Extra Crunch:** Add some toasted nuts or seeds, such as almonds or sunflower seeds.
- **For Added Protein:** Include some grilled chicken or chickpeas.

This Warm Farro Salad is perfect as a hearty side dish or a light main course, with a satisfying combination of textures and flavors!

Watermelon and Feta Salad

1. **Ingredients**:
    1. 4 cups watermelon, cubed
    2. 1 cup feta cheese, crumbled
    3. 1/4 cup fresh mint leaves, chopped
    4. 1/4 cup red onion, thinly sliced
    5. 2 tbsp olive oil
    6. 1 tbsp balsamic vinegar
    7. Salt and pepper to taste
2. **Instructions**:
    1. In a large bowl, combine the watermelon, feta cheese, mint, and red onion.
    2. Drizzle with olive oil and balsamic vinegar.
    3. Gently toss to mix.
    4. Season with salt and pepper to taste.

Enjoy your refreshing salad!

Quinoa and Black Bean Salad

Ingredients:

- **For the Salad:**
    - 1 cup quinoa
    - 2 cups water or vegetable broth (for cooking the quinoa)
    - 1 can (15 oz) black beans, drained and rinsed
    - 1 cup corn kernels (fresh, frozen, or canned)
    - 1 cup cherry tomatoes, halved
    - 1/2 cup diced red bell pepper
    - 1/4 cup red onion, finely chopped
    - 1/4 cup fresh cilantro or parsley, chopped
    - 1 avocado, diced (optional)
- **For the Dressing:**
    - 3 tbsp extra-virgin olive oil
    - 2 tbsp lime juice
    - 1 tbsp apple cider vinegar
    - 1 tsp cumin
    - 1 clove garlic, minced
    - Salt and black pepper to taste

Instructions:

1. **Cook the Quinoa:**
    - Rinse the quinoa under cold water.
    - In a medium pot, bring 2 cups of water or vegetable broth to a boil. Add the quinoa, reduce the heat to low, cover, and simmer for 15 minutes, or until the quinoa is tender and the liquid is absorbed. Fluff with a fork and let it cool.
2. **Prepare the Salad Ingredients:**
    - In a large bowl, combine the cooked quinoa, black beans, corn, cherry tomatoes, diced red bell pepper, and red onion.
    - Add the chopped cilantro or parsley and diced avocado if using.
3. **Make the Dressing:**
    - In a small bowl or jar, whisk together olive oil, lime juice, apple cider vinegar, cumin, minced garlic, salt, and black pepper.
4. **Combine the Salad:**
    - Drizzle the dressing over the quinoa mixture and toss gently to combine.
5. **Serve:**
    - Serve immediately, or refrigerate for about 30 minutes to let the flavors meld.

Tips:

- **For Extra Flavor:** Add a pinch of chili powder or some diced jalapeño for heat.
- **For a Heartier Salad:** Mix in some cooked chicken or tofu.

This Quinoa and Black Bean Salad is a protein-packed, refreshing dish that's great for a light lunch or as a side for dinner!

Chickpea and Cucumber Salad

Ingredients:

- **For the Salad:**
    - 1 can (15 oz) chickpeas, drained and rinsed
    - 1 large cucumber, diced
    - 1 cup cherry tomatoes, halved
    - 1/4 cup red onion, finely chopped
    - 1/4 cup fresh parsley or cilantro, chopped
    - 1/4 cup crumbled feta cheese or goat cheese (optional)
    - 1/4 cup sliced black olives or Kalamata olives (optional)
- **For the Dressing:**
    - 3 tbsp extra-virgin olive oil
    - 2 tbsp lemon juice
    - 1 tbsp red wine vinegar
    - 1 tsp Dijon mustard
    - 1 clove garlic, minced
    - 1/2 tsp dried oregano or thyme
    - Salt and black pepper to taste

Instructions:

1. **Prepare the Salad Ingredients:**
    - In a large bowl, combine the chickpeas, diced cucumber, cherry tomatoes, red onion, and chopped parsley or cilantro.
    - Add crumbled feta cheese or goat cheese and sliced olives if using.
2. **Make the Dressing:**
    - In a small bowl or jar, whisk together olive oil, lemon juice, red wine vinegar, Dijon mustard, minced garlic, dried oregano or thyme, salt, and black pepper.
3. **Combine the Salad:**
    - Drizzle the dressing over the salad and toss gently to coat all ingredients evenly.
4. **Serve:**
    - Serve immediately, or refrigerate for about 30 minutes to let the flavors meld.

Tips:

- **For Extra Crunch:** Add some diced bell peppers or radishes.
- **For a Protein Boost:** Include some grilled chicken or tofu.

This Chickpea and Cucumber Salad is a quick and easy dish that's perfect for a healthy lunch or as a side for dinner!

Spinach and Avocado Salad

Ingredients:

- **For the Salad:**
    - 1 can (15 oz) chickpeas, drained and rinsed
    - 1 large cucumber, diced
    - 1 cup cherry tomatoes, halved
    - 1/4 cup red onion, finely chopped
    - 1/4 cup fresh parsley or cilantro, chopped
    - 1/4 cup crumbled feta cheese or goat cheese (optional)
    - 1/4 cup sliced black olives or Kalamata olives (optional)
- **For the Dressing:**
    - 3 tbsp extra-virgin olive oil
    - 2 tbsp lemon juice
    - 1 tbsp red wine vinegar
    - 1 tsp Dijon mustard
    - 1 clove garlic, minced
    - 1/2 tsp dried oregano or thyme
    - Salt and black pepper to taste

Instructions:

1. **Prepare the Salad Ingredients:**
    - In a large bowl, combine chickpeas, diced cucumber, cherry tomatoes, red onion, and chopped parsley or cilantro.
    - Add crumbled feta cheese or goat cheese and sliced olives if using.
2. **Make the Dressing:**
    - In a small bowl or jar, whisk together olive oil, lemon juice, red wine vinegar, Dijon mustard, minced garlic, dried oregano or thyme, salt, and black pepper.
3. **Combine the Salad:**
    - Drizzle the dressing over the salad and toss gently to coat all ingredients evenly.
4. **Serve:**
    - Serve immediately or refrigerate for about 30 minutes to let the flavors meld.

Spinach and Avocado Salad

Ingredients:

- **For the Salad:**
    - 4 cups fresh spinach leaves
    - 1 ripe avocado, diced
    - 1/2 cup cherry tomatoes, halved
    - 1/4 cup red onion, thinly sliced
    - 1/4 cup sliced almonds or walnuts (optional)
    - 1/4 cup crumbled feta cheese or goat cheese (optional)
    - 1/4 cup fresh basil or cilantro, chopped (optional)
- **For the Dressing:**
    - 3 tbsp extra-virgin olive oil
    - 2 tbsp balsamic vinegar or lemon juice
    - 1 tsp honey or maple syrup
    - 1 tsp Dijon mustard
    - 1 clove garlic, minced
    - Salt and black pepper to taste

Instructions:

1. **Prepare the Salad Ingredients:**
    - In a large bowl, combine fresh spinach leaves, diced avocado, cherry tomatoes, and red onion.
    - Add sliced almonds or walnuts, crumbled feta cheese, and fresh basil or cilantro if using.
2. **Make the Dressing:**
    - In a small bowl or jar, whisk together olive oil, balsamic vinegar or lemon juice, honey or maple syrup, Dijon mustard, minced garlic, salt, and black pepper.
3. **Combine the Salad:**
    - Drizzle the dressing over the salad and toss gently to coat all ingredients evenly.
4. **Serve:**
    - Serve immediately for the freshest taste.

Both salads offer a fresh and flavorful option for lunch or as a side dish. Enjoy!

Roasted Brussels Sprout Salad

Ingredients:

- **For the Salad:**
    - 1 lb Brussels sprouts, trimmed and halved
    - 2 tbsp olive oil
    - 1/2 tsp salt
    - 1/4 tsp black pepper
    - 1/4 cup sliced almonds or walnuts (optional)
    - 1/4 cup dried cranberries or raisins
    - 1/4 cup crumbled feta cheese or goat cheese (optional)
    - 1/4 cup pomegranate seeds (optional)
    - 1/4 cup thinly sliced red onion (optional)
    - 2 cups mixed greens (optional)
- **For the Dressing:**
    - 3 tbsp extra-virgin olive oil
    - 2 tbsp balsamic vinegar
    - 1 tbsp honey or maple syrup
    - 1 tsp Dijon mustard
    - 1 clove garlic, minced
    - Salt and black pepper to taste

Instructions:

1. **Roast the Brussels Sprouts:**
    - Preheat your oven to 400°F (200°C).
    - Toss the halved Brussels sprouts with olive oil, salt, and black pepper.
    - Spread them out in a single layer on a baking sheet.
    - Roast for 20-25 minutes, or until they are crispy on the edges and tender in the center, tossing halfway through.
2. **Prepare the Salad Ingredients:**
    - If using, toast the sliced almonds or walnuts in a dry skillet over medium heat until golden and fragrant, about 3-4 minutes.
    - In a large bowl, combine the roasted Brussels sprouts with dried cranberries or raisins, crumbled feta cheese or goat cheese, pomegranate seeds, sliced red onion, and mixed greens if using.
3. **Make the Dressing:**
    - In a small bowl or jar, whisk together olive oil, balsamic vinegar, honey or maple syrup, Dijon mustard, minced garlic, salt, and black pepper.
4. **Combine the Salad:**
    - Drizzle the dressing over the salad and toss gently to coat all ingredients evenly.
5. **Serve:**

- Serve immediately while the Brussels sprouts are still warm or at room temperature.

Tips:

- **For Extra Crunch:** Add some crispy bacon bits or roasted chickpeas.
- **For a Heartier Salad:** Include some quinoa or farro.

This Roasted Brussels Sprout Salad combines savory roasted sprouts with sweet and tangy elements, creating a balanced and satisfying dish. Enjoy!

Asian Noodle Salad

Ingredients:

- **For the Salad:**
    - 8 oz rice noodles or soba noodles
    - 1 cup shredded carrots
    - 1 cup thinly sliced red cabbage
    - 1 cup snap peas or snow peas, trimmed and sliced
    - 1/2 cup bell pepper, thinly sliced
    - 1/4 cup chopped green onions
    - 1/4 cup fresh cilantro, chopped
    - 1/4 cup sesame seeds (optional)
    - 1/4 cup chopped peanuts or cashews (optional)
- **For the Dressing:**
    - 1/4 cup soy sauce or tamari
    - 2 tbsp rice vinegar
    - 1 tbsp sesame oil
    - 1 tbsp honey or maple syrup
    - 1 tbsp hoisin sauce (optional)
    - 1 clove garlic, minced
    - 1 tsp freshly grated ginger
    - 1 tsp sriracha or red pepper flakes (optional, for heat)

Instructions:

1. **Cook the Noodles:**
    - Cook the noodles according to package instructions. Drain and rinse with cold water to stop cooking and cool the noodles.
2. **Prepare the Salad Ingredients:**
    - In a large bowl, combine the cooked noodles, shredded carrots, sliced red cabbage, snap peas, bell pepper, green onions, and chopped cilantro.
3. **Make the Dressing:**
    - In a small bowl or jar, whisk together soy sauce or tamari, rice vinegar, sesame oil, honey or maple syrup, hoisin sauce (if using), minced garlic, grated ginger, and sriracha or red pepper flakes (if using).
4. **Combine the Salad:**
    - Drizzle the dressing over the noodle mixture and toss gently to coat all ingredients evenly.
5. **Add Toppings:**
    - Sprinkle with sesame seeds and chopped peanuts or cashews if desired.
6. **Serve:**
    - Serve immediately or refrigerate for about 30 minutes to allow the flavors to meld.

Tips:

- **For Extra Protein:** Add some cooked chicken, tofu, or shrimp.
- **For a Fresh Touch:** Add some thinly sliced cucumber or fresh herbs like mint.

This Asian Noodle Salad is a delicious blend of textures and flavors, perfect for a light meal or as a vibrant side dish!

Corn and Tomato Salad

Ingredients:

- **For the Salad:**
    - 2 cups fresh corn kernels (about 3-4 ears of corn) or 1 can (15 oz) of drained corn
    - 2 cups cherry or grape tomatoes, halved
    - 1/2 cup diced red onion
    - 1/4 cup fresh basil or cilantro, chopped
    - 1/4 cup crumbled feta cheese or goat cheese (optional)
    - 1 avocado, diced (optional)
- **For the Dressing:**
    - 3 tbsp extra-virgin olive oil
    - 2 tbsp fresh lime juice or red wine vinegar
    - 1 tbsp honey or maple syrup
    - 1 clove garlic, minced
    - 1/2 tsp ground cumin or smoked paprika (optional)
    - Salt and black pepper to taste

Instructions:

1. **Prepare the Corn:**
    - If using fresh corn, bring a pot of water to a boil. Add the corn and cook for 3-5 minutes until tender. Drain and let cool, then cut the kernels off the cob.
    - If using canned corn, simply drain and rinse.
2. **Prepare the Salad Ingredients:**
    - In a large bowl, combine the corn kernels, halved cherry tomatoes, diced red onion, and chopped fresh basil or cilantro.
    - Add crumbled feta cheese or goat cheese and diced avocado if using.
3. **Make the Dressing:**
    - In a small bowl or jar, whisk together olive oil, lime juice or red wine vinegar, honey or maple syrup, minced garlic, ground cumin or smoked paprika (if using), salt, and black pepper.
4. **Combine the Salad:**
    - Drizzle the dressing over the salad and toss gently to coat all ingredients evenly.
5. **Serve:**
    - Serve immediately, or refrigerate for about 30 minutes to let the flavors meld.

Tips:

- **For Extra Crunch:** Add some diced bell peppers or sliced radishes.
- **For a Hearty Salad:** Mix in some cooked quinoa or beans for added protein.

This Corn and Tomato Salad is perfect as a refreshing side dish or a light meal, showcasing fresh summer flavors and vibrant colors!

Mixed Green Salad with Nuts

Ingredients:

- **For the Salad:**
    - 4 cups mixed salad greens (such as arugula, spinach, and baby kale)
    - 1/2 cup cherry or grape tomatoes, halved
    - 1/2 cup cucumber, sliced
    - 1/4 cup red onion, thinly sliced
    - 1/4 cup nuts (such as almonds, walnuts, or pecans), toasted
    - 1/4 cup crumbled feta cheese or goat cheese (optional)
    - 1/4 cup dried cranberries or raisins (optional)
- **For the Dressing:**
    - 3 tbsp extra-virgin olive oil
    - 2 tbsp balsamic vinegar or lemon juice
    - 1 tbsp honey or maple syrup
    - 1 tsp Dijon mustard
    - 1 clove garlic, minced
    - Salt and black pepper to taste

Instructions:

1. **Prepare the Salad Ingredients:**
    - In a large bowl, combine the mixed greens, cherry tomatoes, cucumber, and red onion.
    - If using, add the toasted nuts, crumbled feta cheese, and dried cranberries or raisins.
2. **Make the Dressing:**
    - In a small bowl or jar, whisk together olive oil, balsamic vinegar or lemon juice, honey or maple syrup, Dijon mustard, minced garlic, salt, and black pepper.
3. **Combine the Salad:**
    - Drizzle the dressing over the salad and toss gently to coat all ingredients evenly.
4. **Serve:**
    - Serve immediately for the freshest taste.

Tips:

- **For Extra Flavor:** Add some sliced apples or pears.
- **For a Protein Boost:** Include some grilled chicken or chickpeas.

This Mixed Green Salad with Nuts is a versatile and satisfying dish, perfect as a side or a light main course!

Sweet Corn and Avocado Salad

Ingredients:

- **For the Salad:**
    - 2 cups fresh corn kernels (about 3-4 ears of corn) or 1 can (15 oz) of drained corn
    - 1 ripe avocado, diced
    - 1 cup cherry or grape tomatoes, halved
    - 1/2 cup red onion, finely chopped
    - 1/4 cup fresh cilantro or basil, chopped
    - 1/4 cup crumbled feta cheese or goat cheese (optional)
    - 1/4 cup sliced black olives or Kalamata olives (optional)
- **For the Dressing:**
    - 3 tbsp extra-virgin olive oil
    - 2 tbsp fresh lime juice or red wine vinegar
    - 1 tbsp honey or maple syrup
    - 1 clove garlic, minced
    - 1/2 tsp ground cumin or smoked paprika (optional)
    - Salt and black pepper to taste

Instructions:

1. **Prepare the Corn:**
    - If using fresh corn, bring a pot of water to a boil. Add the corn and cook for 3-5 minutes until tender. Drain and let cool, then cut the kernels off the cob.
    - If using canned corn, simply drain and rinse.
2. **Prepare the Salad Ingredients:**
    - In a large bowl, combine the corn kernels, diced avocado, cherry tomatoes, and red onion.
    - Add the chopped fresh cilantro or basil, crumbled feta cheese, and sliced olives if using.
3. **Make the Dressing:**
    - In a small bowl or jar, whisk together olive oil, lime juice or red wine vinegar, honey or maple syrup, minced garlic, ground cumin or smoked paprika (if using), salt, and black pepper.
4. **Combine the Salad:**
    - Drizzle the dressing over the salad and toss gently to coat all ingredients evenly.
5. **Serve:**
    - Serve immediately for the freshest taste or chill for about 30 minutes to let the flavors meld.

Tips:

- **For Extra Crunch:** Add some diced bell peppers or radishes.
- **For a Heartier Salad:** Mix in some cooked quinoa or beans for added protein.

This Sweet Corn and Avocado Salad is perfect for a summer meal or as a colorful side dish at any time of year!

Edamame and Carrot Salad

Ingredients:

- **For the Salad:**
    - 1 cup shelled edamame (fresh or frozen)
    - 2 large carrots, peeled and julienned or shredded
    - 1/2 cup red bell pepper, thinly sliced
    - 1/4 cup green onions, sliced
    - 1/4 cup fresh cilantro or parsley, chopped
    - 1/4 cup sesame seeds or toasted pumpkin seeds (optional)
    - 1/4 cup crumbled feta cheese or goat cheese (optional)
- **For the Dressing:**
    - 3 tbsp extra-virgin olive oil
    - 2 tbsp rice vinegar or lime juice
    - 1 tbsp soy sauce or tamari
    - 1 tbsp honey or maple syrup
    - 1 tsp grated ginger
    - 1 clove garlic, minced
    - 1/2 tsp sesame oil (optional)
    - Salt and black pepper to taste

Instructions:

1. **Prepare the Edamame:**
    - If using frozen edamame, cook according to package instructions, usually by boiling or steaming. Drain and let cool.
    - If using fresh edamame, blanch in boiling water for about 3-4 minutes, then drain and cool.
2. **Prepare the Salad Ingredients:**
    - In a large bowl, combine the cooked edamame, julienned or shredded carrots, red bell pepper, and green onions.
    - Add the chopped cilantro or parsley and sprinkle with sesame seeds or toasted pumpkin seeds if using. Add crumbled feta cheese if desired.
3. **Make the Dressing:**
    - In a small bowl or jar, whisk together olive oil, rice vinegar or lime juice, soy sauce or tamari, honey or maple syrup, grated ginger, minced garlic, and sesame oil if using. Season with salt and black pepper to taste.
4. **Combine the Salad:**
    - Drizzle the dressing over the salad and toss gently to coat all ingredients evenly.
5. **Serve:**
    - Serve immediately or refrigerate for about 30 minutes to let the flavors meld.

Tips:

- **For Extra Texture:** Add some thinly sliced radishes or cucumber.
- **For a Protein Boost:** Include some grilled chicken or tofu.

This Edamame and Carrot Salad is a crunchy, satisfying option that works well as a side dish or a light main course!

Roasted Butternut Squash Salad

Ingredients:

- **For the Salad:**
    - 1 medium butternut squash, peeled, seeded, and cubed
    - 2 tbsp olive oil
    - Salt and black pepper to taste
    - 1/4 cup crumbled feta cheese or goat cheese
    - 1/4 cup toasted pecans or walnuts
    - 1/4 cup dried cranberries or raisins
    - 2 cups mixed salad greens (such as spinach, arugula, or baby kale)
    - 1/4 cup red onion, thinly sliced (optional)
- **For the Dressing:**
    - 3 tbsp extra-virgin olive oil
    - 2 tbsp balsamic vinegar
    - 1 tbsp maple syrup or honey
    - 1 tsp Dijon mustard
    - 1 clove garlic, minced
    - Salt and black pepper to taste

Instructions:

1. **Roast the Butternut Squash:**
    - Preheat your oven to 400°F (200°C).
    - Toss the butternut squash cubes with olive oil, salt, and black pepper.
    - Spread them out in a single layer on a baking sheet.
    - Roast for 25-30 minutes, or until tender and caramelized, turning halfway through. Let cool slightly.
2. **Prepare the Salad Ingredients:**
    - In a large bowl, combine the mixed salad greens, roasted butternut squash, crumbled feta or goat cheese, toasted pecans or walnuts, dried cranberries or raisins, and red onion if using.
3. **Make the Dressing:**
    - In a small bowl or jar, whisk together olive oil, balsamic vinegar, maple syrup or honey, Dijon mustard, minced garlic, salt, and black pepper.
4. **Combine the Salad:**
    - Drizzle the dressing over the salad and toss gently to coat all ingredients evenly.
5. **Serve:**
    - Serve immediately or refrigerate for about 30 minutes to let the flavors meld.

Tips:

- **For Extra Flavor:** Add some roasted chickpeas or apple slices.
- **For a Heartier Salad:** Include some cooked quinoa or farro.

This Roasted Butternut Squash Salad is a wonderful mix of sweet, savory, and crunchy elements, perfect for a satisfying side dish or a light main course!

Cabbage and Apple Slaw

Ingredients:

- **For the Slaw:**
    - 4 cups shredded cabbage (green, red, or a mix)
    - 1 large apple, cored and julienned or thinly sliced
    - 1/4 cup shredded carrots
    - 1/4 cup thinly sliced red onion
    - 1/4 cup fresh parsley or cilantro, chopped
    - 1/4 cup toasted sunflower seeds or sliced almonds (optional)
    - 1/4 cup dried cranberries or raisins (optional)
- **For the Dressing:**
    - 1/4 cup mayonnaise (or Greek yogurt for a lighter option)
    - 2 tbsp apple cider vinegar
    - 1 tbsp honey or maple syrup
    - 1 tsp Dijon mustard
    - 1 clove garlic, minced (optional)
    - Salt and black pepper to taste

Instructions:

1. **Prepare the Slaw Ingredients:**
    - In a large bowl, combine shredded cabbage, julienned apple, shredded carrots, and thinly sliced red onion.
    - Add the chopped parsley or cilantro, and toss in toasted sunflower seeds or sliced almonds and dried cranberries or raisins if using.
2. **Make the Dressing:**
    - In a small bowl, whisk together mayonnaise (or Greek yogurt), apple cider vinegar, honey or maple syrup, Dijon mustard, minced garlic (if using), salt, and black pepper.
3. **Combine the Slaw:**
    - Drizzle the dressing over the cabbage mixture and toss gently to coat all ingredients evenly.
4. **Serve:**
    - Serve immediately, or refrigerate for about 30 minutes to let the flavors meld and the slaw to chill.

Tips:

- **For Extra Crunch:** Add some thinly sliced radishes or bell peppers.
- **For a Tangier Slaw:** Increase the amount of apple cider vinegar or add a splash of lemon juice.

This Cabbage and Apple Slaw is a refreshing and crunchy side dish that pairs well with a variety of meals, from barbecues to everyday dinners!

Pomegranate and Kale Salad

Ingredients:

- **For the Salad:**
    - 4 cups kale, stems removed and leaves chopped
    - 1 cup pomegranate seeds
    - 1/2 cup crumbled feta cheese or goat cheese
    - 1/4 cup sliced almonds or walnuts, toasted
    - 1/4 cup thinly sliced red onion
    - 1/2 cup cooked quinoa or farro (optional for added protein)
- **For the Dressing:**
    - 3 tbsp extra-virgin olive oil
    - 2 tbsp apple cider vinegar or lemon juice
    - 1 tbsp honey or maple syrup
    - 1 tsp Dijon mustard
    - 1 clove garlic, minced
    - Salt and black pepper to taste

Instructions:

1. **Prepare the Kale:**
    - In a large bowl, massage the chopped kale with a little olive oil and a pinch of salt for about 2-3 minutes until the leaves are tender and reduced in volume.
2. **Prepare the Salad Ingredients:**
    - Add the pomegranate seeds, crumbled feta or goat cheese, toasted almonds or walnuts, and thinly sliced red onion to the kale. If using, add the cooked quinoa or farro.
3. **Make the Dressing:**
    - In a small bowl or jar, whisk together olive oil, apple cider vinegar or lemon juice, honey or maple syrup, Dijon mustard, minced garlic, salt, and black pepper.
4. **Combine the Salad:**
    - Drizzle the dressing over the salad and toss gently to coat all ingredients evenly.
5. **Serve:**
    - Serve immediately or refrigerate for about 30 minutes to let the flavors meld.

Tips:

- **For Extra Freshness:** Add some sliced cucumber or apple.
- **For More Crunch:** Include some roasted chickpeas or sunflower seeds.

This Pomegranate and Kale Salad offers a delightful mix of sweet, tangy, and crunchy textures, making it a perfect side dish or light main course!

Red Bean and Quinoa Salad

Ingredients:

- **For the Salad:**
    - 1 cup quinoa, rinsed
    - 1 can (15 oz) red kidney beans, drained and rinsed
    - 1 cup cherry or grape tomatoes, halved
    - 1/2 cup diced red bell pepper
    - 1/4 cup chopped red onion
    - 1/4 cup chopped fresh cilantro or parsley
    - 1/4 cup crumbled feta cheese or goat cheese (optional)
    - 1 avocado, diced (optional)
- **For the Dressing:**
    - 3 tbsp extra-virgin olive oil
    - 2 tbsp lime juice or red wine vinegar
    - 1 tbsp honey or maple syrup
    - 1 tsp ground cumin or paprika (optional)
    - 1 clove garlic, minced
    - Salt and black pepper to taste

Instructions:

1. **Cook the Quinoa:**
    - In a medium saucepan, combine the quinoa with 2 cups of water. Bring to a boil, then reduce the heat to low, cover, and simmer for about 15 minutes, or until the quinoa is tender and the water is absorbed. Fluff with a fork and let cool.
2. **Prepare the Salad Ingredients:**
    - In a large bowl, combine the cooked quinoa, red kidney beans, cherry tomatoes, diced red bell pepper, and chopped red onion.
    - Add the chopped cilantro or parsley and crumbled feta cheese if using. Add diced avocado if desired.
3. **Make the Dressing:**
    - In a small bowl or jar, whisk together olive oil, lime juice or red wine vinegar, honey or maple syrup, ground cumin or paprika (if using), minced garlic, salt, and black pepper.
4. **Combine the Salad:**
    - Drizzle the dressing over the salad and toss gently to coat all ingredients evenly.
5. **Serve:**
    - Serve immediately or chill in the refrigerator for about 30 minutes to let the flavors meld.

Tips:

- **For Extra Crunch:** Add some diced cucumber or roasted nuts.
- **For a Spicier Kick:** Incorporate some chopped jalapeño or hot sauce into the dressing.

This Red Bean and Quinoa Salad is a hearty and flavorful dish, perfect for a light lunch or a satisfying side!

Roasted Red Pepper Salad

Ingredients:

- **For the Salad:**
    - 4 large red bell peppers
    - 1 cup cherry or grape tomatoes, halved
    - 1/4 cup thinly sliced red onion
    - 1/4 cup Kalamata olives or black olives, pitted and sliced
    - 1/4 cup crumbled feta cheese or goat cheese
    - 2 tbsp fresh basil or parsley, chopped
- **For the Dressing:**
    - 3 tbsp extra-virgin olive oil
    - 2 tbsp red wine vinegar or balsamic vinegar
    - 1 tbsp lemon juice
    - 1 tsp Dijon mustard
    - 1 clove garlic, minced
    - 1/2 tsp dried oregano or Italian seasoning (optional)
    - Salt and black pepper to taste

Instructions:

1. **Roast the Red Peppers:**
    - Preheat your oven to 450°F (230°C).
    - Place the whole red bell peppers on a baking sheet. Roast for 20-30 minutes, turning occasionally, until the skins are charred and blistered.
    - Transfer the peppers to a bowl, cover with plastic wrap, and let steam for about 10 minutes. Peel off the skins, remove the seeds, and slice the peppers into strips.
2. **Prepare the Salad Ingredients:**
    - In a large bowl, combine the roasted red pepper strips, cherry tomatoes, sliced red onion, and olives.
    - Add the crumbled feta cheese and chopped basil or parsley.
3. **Make the Dressing:**
    - In a small bowl or jar, whisk together olive oil, red wine vinegar or balsamic vinegar, lemon juice, Dijon mustard, minced garlic, dried oregano or Italian seasoning (if using), salt, and black pepper.
4. **Combine the Salad:**
    - Drizzle the dressing over the salad and toss gently to coat all ingredients evenly.
5. **Serve:**
    - Serve immediately at room temperature or chilled.

Tips:

- **For Extra Flavor:** Add some capers or a sprinkle of pine nuts.
- **For a Heartier Salad:** Include some cooked quinoa or chickpeas.

This Roasted Red Pepper Salad is a flavorful and visually appealing dish, perfect as a side or a light main course!

Pear and Gorgonzola Salad

Ingredients:

- **For the Salad:**
    - 4 cups mixed greens (such as spinach, arugula, and baby greens)
    - 2 ripe pears, cored and sliced
    - 1/4 cup crumbled Gorgonzola cheese
    - 1/4 cup toasted walnuts or pecans
    - 1/4 cup dried cranberries or pomegranate seeds
    - 1/4 cup thinly sliced red onion (optional)
- **For the Dressing:**
    - 3 tbsp extra-virgin olive oil
    - 2 tbsp balsamic vinegar or red wine vinegar
    - 1 tbsp honey or maple syrup
    - 1 tsp Dijon mustard
    - 1 clove garlic, minced
    - Salt and black pepper to taste

Instructions:

1. **Prepare the Salad Ingredients:**
    - In a large bowl, combine mixed greens, sliced pears, crumbled Gorgonzola cheese, toasted walnuts or pecans, dried cranberries or pomegranate seeds, and thinly sliced red onion if using.
2. **Make the Dressing:**
    - In a small bowl or jar, whisk together olive oil, balsamic vinegar or red wine vinegar, honey or maple syrup, Dijon mustard, minced garlic, salt, and black pepper.
3. **Combine the Salad:**
    - Drizzle the dressing over the salad and toss gently to coat all ingredients evenly.
4. **Serve:**
    - Serve immediately for the freshest taste.

Tips:

- **For Added Crunch:** Include some sliced apples or a sprinkle of toasted seeds.
- **For Extra Protein:** Add some grilled chicken or chickpeas.

This Pear and Gorgonzola Salad is a delightful blend of sweet and savory flavors, perfect as a sophisticated side dish or a light main course!

Fennel and Orange Salad

Ingredients:

- **For the Salad:**
    - 1 large fennel bulb, thinly sliced
    - 2 large oranges, peeled and segmented
    - 1/4 cup red onion, thinly sliced
    - 1/4 cup black olives or Kalamata olives, pitted and sliced
    - 1/4 cup crumbled feta cheese or goat cheese (optional)
    - 2 tbsp fresh dill or parsley, chopped
- **For the Dressing:**
    - 3 tbsp extra-virgin olive oil
    - 2 tbsp fresh lemon juice or white wine vinegar
    - 1 tsp honey or maple syrup
    - 1 tsp Dijon mustard
    - 1 clove garlic, minced
    - Salt and black pepper to taste

Instructions:

1. **Prepare the Salad Ingredients:**
    - In a large bowl, combine the thinly sliced fennel, orange segments, red onion, and sliced olives.
    - Add the crumbled feta cheese and chopped dill or parsley.
2. **Make the Dressing:**
    - In a small bowl or jar, whisk together olive oil, lemon juice or white wine vinegar, honey or maple syrup, Dijon mustard, minced garlic, salt, and black pepper.
3. **Combine the Salad:**
    - Drizzle the dressing over the salad and toss gently to coat all ingredients evenly.
4. **Serve:**
    - Serve immediately, or chill for about 30 minutes to let the flavors meld.

Tips:

- **For Extra Texture:** Add some toasted pine nuts or sunflower seeds.
- **For a Touch of Sweetness:** Include some thinly sliced apple or pear.

This Fennel and Orange Salad is a delightful mix of crisp and juicy elements, making it a refreshing side dish or a light main course!

Grilled Peach Salad

Ingredients:

- **For the Salad:**
    - 4 ripe peaches, halved and pitted
    - 4 cups mixed greens (such as arugula, spinach, and baby kale)
    - 1/4 cup crumbled goat cheese or feta cheese
    - 1/4 cup toasted pecans or walnuts
    - 1/4 cup thinly sliced red onion
    - 1/4 cup dried cranberries or pomegranate seeds (optional)
- **For the Dressing:**
    - 3 tbsp extra-virgin olive oil
    - 2 tbsp balsamic vinegar
    - 1 tbsp honey or maple syrup
    - 1 tsp Dijon mustard
    - 1 clove garlic, minced
    - Salt and black pepper to taste

Instructions:

1. **Grill the Peaches:**
    - Preheat your grill to medium-high heat.
    - Lightly brush the peach halves with olive oil.
    - Grill the peaches for 2-3 minutes per side, or until grill marks appear and they are slightly softened. Remove from the grill and let cool slightly, then slice into wedges.
2. **Prepare the Salad Ingredients:**
    - In a large bowl, combine the mixed greens, crumbled goat cheese or feta cheese, toasted pecans or walnuts, and thinly sliced red onion.
    - Add the grilled peach slices and dried cranberries or pomegranate seeds if using.
3. **Make the Dressing:**
    - In a small bowl or jar, whisk together olive oil, balsamic vinegar, honey or maple syrup, Dijon mustard, minced garlic, salt, and black pepper.
4. **Combine the Salad:**
    - Drizzle the dressing over the salad and toss gently to coat all ingredients evenly.
5. **Serve:**
    - Serve immediately for the freshest taste.

Tips:

- **For Extra Flavor:** Add some sliced avocado or a sprinkle of fresh herbs like basil or mint.

- **For a Heartier Salad:** Include some grilled chicken or quinoa.

This Grilled Peach Salad combines the sweetness of peaches with savory and crunchy elements, making it a delicious and visually appealing dish!

Spinach and Mushroom Salad

Ingredients:

- **For the Salad:**
    - 4 cups fresh spinach leaves
    - 1 cup mushrooms, sliced (button, cremini, or your choice)
    - 1/4 cup thinly sliced red onion
    - 1/4 cup crumbled feta cheese or goat cheese
    - 1/4 cup toasted pine nuts or sliced almonds
    - 1/4 cup dried cranberries or raisins (optional)
- **For the Dressing:**
    - 3 tbsp extra-virgin olive oil
    - 2 tbsp balsamic vinegar or red wine vinegar
    - 1 tbsp Dijon mustard
    - 1 tsp honey or maple syrup
    - 1 clove garlic, minced
    - Salt and black pepper to taste

Instructions:

1. **Sauté the Mushrooms:**
    - In a skillet over medium heat, add a little olive oil.
    - Sauté the sliced mushrooms for about 5-7 minutes, or until tender and golden brown. Season with a pinch of salt and pepper. Let cool.
2. **Prepare the Salad Ingredients:**
    - In a large bowl, combine the fresh spinach leaves, sautéed mushrooms, thinly sliced red onion, and crumbled feta or goat cheese.
    - Add the toasted pine nuts or sliced almonds and dried cranberries or raisins if using.
3. **Make the Dressing:**
    - In a small bowl or jar, whisk together olive oil, balsamic vinegar or red wine vinegar, Dijon mustard, honey or maple syrup, minced garlic, salt, and black pepper.
4. **Combine the Salad:**
    - Drizzle the dressing over the salad and toss gently to coat all ingredients evenly.
5. **Serve:**
    - Serve immediately or refrigerate for a short time to let the flavors meld.

Tips:

- **For Extra Flavor:** Add some sliced avocado or grilled chicken.
- **For a Warm Salad:** Serve the sautéed mushrooms slightly warm over the spinach.

This Spinach and Mushroom Salad is a savory and satisfying option, perfect as a light lunch or a side dish!

Chickpea and Red Pepper Salad

Ingredients:

- **For the Salad:**
    - 1 can (15 oz) chickpeas, drained and rinsed
    - 1 large red bell pepper, diced
    - 1/2 cup cherry or grape tomatoes, halved
    - 1/4 cup thinly sliced red onion
    - 1/4 cup chopped fresh parsley or cilantro
    - 1/4 cup crumbled feta cheese or goat cheese (optional)
    - 1/4 cup black olives or Kalamata olives, pitted and sliced (optional)
- **For the Dressing:**
    - 3 tbsp extra-virgin olive oil
    - 2 tbsp lemon juice or red wine vinegar
    - 1 tbsp Dijon mustard
    - 1 tsp honey or maple syrup
    - 1 clove garlic, minced
    - Salt and black pepper to taste

Instructions:

1. **Prepare the Salad Ingredients:**
    - In a large bowl, combine chickpeas, diced red bell pepper, cherry tomatoes, thinly sliced red onion, and chopped parsley or cilantro.
    - Add crumbled feta cheese and sliced olives if using.
2. **Make the Dressing:**
    - In a small bowl or jar, whisk together olive oil, lemon juice or red wine vinegar, Dijon mustard, honey or maple syrup, minced garlic, salt, and black pepper.
3. **Combine the Salad:**
    - Drizzle the dressing over the salad and toss gently to coat all ingredients evenly.
4. **Serve:**
    - Serve immediately or chill for about 30 minutes to allow flavors to meld.

Tips:

- **For Extra Crunch:** Add some diced cucumber or roasted nuts.
- **For a Heartier Salad:** Include some cooked quinoa or grilled chicken.

This Chickpea and Red Pepper Salad is refreshing and nutritious, perfect as a light meal or a satisfying side dish!

Avocado and Citrus Salad

Ingredients:

- **For the Salad:**
    - 2 ripe avocados, peeled, pitted, and sliced
    - 2 large oranges, peeled and segmented
    - 1 large grapefruit, peeled and segmented
    - 1/4 cup thinly sliced red onion
    - 1/4 cup chopped fresh mint or cilantro
    - 1/4 cup crumbled feta cheese or goat cheese (optional)
    - 1/4 cup toasted pistachios or almonds (optional)
- **For the Dressing:**
    - 3 tbsp extra-virgin olive oil
    - 2 tbsp fresh lime juice or white wine vinegar
    - 1 tbsp honey or agave syrup
    - 1 tsp Dijon mustard
    - Salt and black pepper to taste

Instructions:

1. **Prepare the Salad Ingredients:**
    - In a large bowl, gently combine the sliced avocados, orange segments, grapefruit segments, and thinly sliced red onion.
    - Add the chopped mint or cilantro, and crumbled feta cheese and toasted pistachios or almonds if using.
2. **Make the Dressing:**
    - In a small bowl or jar, whisk together olive oil, lime juice or white wine vinegar, honey or agave syrup, Dijon mustard, salt, and black pepper.
3. **Combine the Salad:**
    - Drizzle the dressing over the salad and toss gently to coat all ingredients evenly.
4. **Serve:**
    - Serve immediately to keep the avocado fresh and creamy.

Tips:

- **For Extra Crunch:** Add some sliced cucumber or radishes.
- **For a Touch of Heat:** Include a pinch of chili flakes in the dressing.

This Avocado and Citrus Salad offers a delightful mix of creamy, tangy, and refreshing flavors, making it perfect as a light main course or a vibrant side dish!

Mediterranean Couscous Salad

Ingredients:

- **For the Salad:**
    - 1 cup couscous (preferably whole wheat or regular)
    - 1 cup cherry or grape tomatoes, halved
    - 1/2 cup cucumber, diced
    - 1/4 cup red onion, finely chopped
    - 1/4 cup Kalamata olives, pitted and sliced
    - 1/4 cup crumbled feta cheese
    - 1/4 cup chopped fresh parsley or mint
    - 1/4 cup diced red bell pepper (optional)
    - 1/4 cup chickpeas, drained and rinsed (optional)
- **For the Dressing:**
    - 3 tbsp extra-virgin olive oil
    - 2 tbsp lemon juice
    - 1 tbsp red wine vinegar
    - 1 tsp Dijon mustard
    - 1 clove garlic, minced
    - 1/2 tsp dried oregano or Italian seasoning
    - Salt and black pepper to taste

Instructions:

1. **Cook the Couscous:**
    - In a medium saucepan, bring 1 cup of water to a boil. Stir in the couscous, cover, and remove from heat. Let it sit for 5 minutes, then fluff with a fork and let it cool.
2. **Prepare the Salad Ingredients:**
    - In a large bowl, combine the cooked and cooled couscous, cherry tomatoes, cucumber, red onion, olives, feta cheese, and chopped parsley or mint.
    - If using, add the diced red bell pepper and chickpeas.
3. **Make the Dressing:**
    - In a small bowl or jar, whisk together olive oil, lemon juice, red wine vinegar, Dijon mustard, minced garlic, dried oregano or Italian seasoning, salt, and black pepper.
4. **Combine the Salad:**
    - Drizzle the dressing over the couscous mixture and toss gently to coat all ingredients evenly.
5. **Serve:**
    - Serve immediately or refrigerate for about 30 minutes to let the flavors meld.

Tips:

- **For Extra Crunch:** Add some diced avocado or a sprinkle of toasted pine nuts.
- **For a Heartier Salad:** Include some grilled chicken or shrimp.

This Mediterranean Couscous Salad is a flavorful and satisfying dish, perfect as a refreshing side or a light main course!

Herb and Tomato Salad

Ingredients:

- **For the Salad:**
    - 4 cups ripe cherry or grape tomatoes, halved
    - 1 cup fresh basil leaves, torn or chopped
    - 1/2 cup fresh parsley, chopped
    - 1/4 cup fresh chives or green onions, chopped
    - 1/4 cup crumbled feta cheese or goat cheese (optional)
    - 1/4 cup thinly sliced red onion (optional)
    - 1/4 cup black olives or Kalamata olives, pitted and sliced (optional)
- **For the Dressing:**
    - 3 tbsp extra-virgin olive oil
    - 2 tbsp balsamic vinegar or red wine vinegar
    - 1 tsp Dijon mustard
    - 1 clove garlic, minced
    - 1 tsp honey or maple syrup
    - Salt and black pepper to taste

Instructions:

1. **Prepare the Salad Ingredients:**
    - In a large bowl, combine the halved cherry or grape tomatoes with the fresh basil, parsley, and chives or green onions.
    - Add the crumbled feta cheese, thinly sliced red onion, and olives if using.
2. **Make the Dressing:**
    - In a small bowl or jar, whisk together olive oil, balsamic vinegar or red wine vinegar, Dijon mustard, minced garlic, honey or maple syrup, salt, and black pepper.
3. **Combine the Salad:**
    - Drizzle the dressing over the tomato and herb mixture and toss gently to coat all ingredients evenly.
4. **Serve:**
    - Serve immediately for the freshest taste.

Tips:

- **For Extra Freshness:** Add some sliced cucumber or avocado.
- **For Added Crunch:** Include some toasted pine nuts or sunflower seeds.

This Herb and Tomato Salad is a refreshing and aromatic dish, perfect as a light lunch or a vibrant side for any meal!

Roasted Cauliflower Salad

Ingredients:

For the Salad:

- 1 large head of cauliflower, cut into florets
- 2 tbsp olive oil
- Salt and freshly ground black pepper, to taste
- 1/2 tsp smoked paprika (optional, for extra flavor)
- 1/4 tsp ground cumin (optional, for extra flavor)
- 1 cup cherry tomatoes, halved
- 1/2 red onion, thinly sliced
- 1/4 cup Kalamata olives, pitted and sliced
- 1/4 cup crumbled feta cheese
- 1/4 cup chopped fresh parsley

For the Dressing:

- 3 tbsp olive oil
- 2 tbsp lemon juice
- 1 tbsp red wine vinegar
- 1 clove garlic, minced
- 1 tsp Dijon mustard
- 1/2 tsp honey or maple syrup (optional, for a touch of sweetness)
- Salt and freshly ground black pepper, to taste

Instructions:

1. **Preheat Oven:** Preheat your oven to 425°F (220°C).
2. **Roast the Cauliflower:**
   - Toss the cauliflower florets with olive oil, salt, pepper, smoked paprika, and ground cumin.
   - Spread the cauliflower out in a single layer on a baking sheet.
   - Roast for 20-25 minutes, or until the cauliflower is tender and golden brown, tossing halfway through for even roasting.
3. **Prepare the Dressing:**
   - In a small bowl, whisk together the olive oil, lemon juice, red wine vinegar, minced garlic, Dijon mustard, and honey (if using).
   - Season with salt and pepper to taste.
4. **Assemble the Salad:**
   - In a large bowl, combine the roasted cauliflower, cherry tomatoes, red onion, olives, and feta cheese.
   - Pour the dressing over the salad and toss gently to coat.

5. **Finish and Serve:**
    - Sprinkle the chopped parsley over the top.
    - Serve warm or at room temperature.

Enjoy your roasted cauliflower salad!

Green Bean and Almond Salad

Ingredients:

For the Salad:

- 1 lb (450 g) fresh green beans, trimmed and cut into bite-sized pieces
- 1/2 cup sliced almonds (toasted if desired)
- 1/4 cup thinly sliced red onion
- 1/4 cup crumbled feta cheese (optional)
- 1/4 cup chopped fresh parsley or basil (for garnish)

For the Dressing:

- 3 tbsp olive oil
- 2 tbsp lemon juice
- 1 tbsp Dijon mustard
- 1 clove garlic, minced
- 1 tsp honey or maple syrup (optional, for a touch of sweetness)
- Salt and freshly ground black pepper, to taste

Instructions:

1. **Blanch the Green Beans:**
    - Bring a large pot of salted water to a boil.
    - Add the green beans and cook for 3-4 minutes, or until tender-crisp.
    - Immediately transfer the green beans to a bowl of ice water to stop the cooking process. After a few minutes, drain and pat dry with a paper towel.
2. **Prepare the Dressing:**
    - In a small bowl, whisk together the olive oil, lemon juice, Dijon mustard, minced garlic, and honey (if using).
    - Season with salt and pepper to taste.
3. **Assemble the Salad:**
    - In a large bowl, combine the blanched green beans, sliced almonds, red onion, and crumbled feta cheese (if using).
    - Pour the dressing over the salad and toss gently to coat.
4. **Garnish and Serve:**
    - Sprinkle the chopped parsley or basil over the top.
    - Serve immediately or chill in the refrigerator for 30 minutes to allow flavors to meld.

This salad is fresh, crunchy, and full of flavor. Enjoy!

Sweet Potato and Kale Salad

Ingredients:

For the Salad:

- 2 medium sweet potatoes, peeled and cubed
- 1 tbsp olive oil
- Salt and freshly ground black pepper, to taste
- 1/2 tsp ground cinnamon (optional, for added warmth)
- 1 bunch kale, stems removed and leaves chopped
- 1/4 cup dried cranberries
- 1/4 cup chopped walnuts or pecans (toasted if desired)
- 1/4 cup crumbled goat cheese or feta cheese

For the Dressing:

- 3 tbsp olive oil
- 2 tbsp apple cider vinegar
- 1 tbsp maple syrup or honey
- 1 tsp Dijon mustard
- 1 clove garlic, minced
- Salt and freshly ground black pepper, to taste

Instructions:

1. **Roast the Sweet Potatoes:**
    - Preheat your oven to 400°F (200°C).
    - Toss the sweet potato cubes with olive oil, salt, pepper, and cinnamon (if using).
    - Spread them out in a single layer on a baking sheet and roast for 25-30 minutes, or until tender and slightly caramelized, tossing halfway through.
2. **Prepare the Dressing:**
    - In a small bowl, whisk together the olive oil, apple cider vinegar, maple syrup or honey, Dijon mustard, and minced garlic.
    - Season with salt and pepper to taste.
3. **Massage the Kale:**
    - In a large bowl, add the chopped kale.
    - Drizzle a small amount of olive oil over the kale and massage it with your hands for a few minutes until it becomes tender.
4. **Assemble the Salad:**
    - Add the roasted sweet potatoes, dried cranberries, and chopped nuts to the kale.
    - Pour the dressing over the salad and toss gently to coat.
    - Sprinkle with crumbled cheese.
5. **Serve:**

- Serve immediately or let it sit for a few minutes to allow flavors to meld.

This salad is a great balance of sweet and savory, with a satisfying crunch. Enjoy!

Brussels Sprout and Bacon Salad

Ingredients:

For the Salad:

- 1 lb (450 g) Brussels sprouts, trimmed and thinly sliced
- 6 slices bacon, chopped
- 1/4 cup chopped pecans or walnuts (toasted if desired)
- 1/4 cup dried cranberries or raisins
- 1/4 cup shaved Parmesan cheese

For the Dressing:

- 3 tbsp olive oil
- 2 tbsp apple cider vinegar
- 1 tbsp Dijon mustard
- 1 tbsp maple syrup or honey
- 1 clove garlic, minced
- Salt and freshly ground black pepper, to taste

Instructions:

1. **Cook the Bacon:**
    - In a large skillet over medium heat, cook the chopped bacon until crispy.
    - Remove the bacon with a slotted spoon and drain on paper towels.
2. **Sauté the Brussels Sprouts:**
    - In the same skillet with a bit of bacon drippings, sauté the sliced Brussels sprouts for 4-5 minutes until tender and slightly caramelized.
    - Transfer the sprouts to a large bowl.
3. **Prepare the Dressing:**
    - In a small bowl, whisk together olive oil, apple cider vinegar, Dijon mustard, maple syrup or honey, and minced garlic.
    - Season with salt and pepper to taste.
4. **Assemble the Salad:**
    - Add the cooked bacon, chopped nuts, dried cranberries, and shaved Parmesan to the Brussels sprouts.
    - Pour the dressing over the salad and toss gently to combine.
5. **Serve:**
    - Serve warm or at room temperature.

This salad combines the richness of bacon with the freshness of Brussels sprouts, making it a tasty and satisfying dish. Enjoy!

Avocado and Black Bean Quinoa Salad

Ingredients:

For the Salad:

- 1 cup quinoa (uncooked)
- 1 can (15 oz) black beans, drained and rinsed
- 1 cup corn kernels (fresh, frozen, or canned)
- 1 large avocado, diced
- 1 red bell pepper, diced
- 1/2 red onion, finely chopped
- 1/4 cup chopped fresh cilantro
- 1/2 cup crumbled feta cheese (optional)

For the Dressing:

- 3 tbsp olive oil
- 2 tbsp lime juice
- 1 tbsp red wine vinegar
- 1 tsp honey or maple syrup (optional, for a touch of sweetness)
- 1 clove garlic, minced
- 1/2 tsp ground cumin
- Salt and freshly ground black pepper, to taste

Instructions:

1. **Cook the Quinoa:**
   - Rinse the quinoa under cold water.
   - In a medium saucepan, combine the quinoa with 2 cups of water (or vegetable broth for more flavor).
   - Bring to a boil, then reduce the heat to low, cover, and simmer for 15 minutes, or until the quinoa is tender and the water is absorbed.
   - Remove from heat and let it sit, covered, for 5 minutes. Fluff with a fork and let it cool.
2. **Prepare the Dressing:**
   - In a small bowl, whisk together the olive oil, lime juice, red wine vinegar, honey (if using), minced garlic, ground cumin, salt, and pepper.
3. **Assemble the Salad:**
   - In a large bowl, combine the cooked quinoa, black beans, corn, avocado, red bell pepper, red onion, and cilantro.
   - Pour the dressing over the salad and toss gently to combine.
   - If using, sprinkle the crumbled feta cheese on top.
4. **Serve:**

- Serve immediately or chill in the refrigerator for 30 minutes to let the flavors meld.

This salad is not only delicious but also packed with protein, healthy fats, and fresh veggies. Enjoy!

Beet and Orange Salad

Ingredients:

For the Salad:

- 4 medium beets, peeled and cut into wedges
- 2 large oranges, peeled and segmented
- 1/4 cup thinly sliced red onion
- 1/4 cup crumbled goat cheese or feta cheese
- 1/4 cup chopped walnuts or pecans (toasted if desired)
- 2 cups mixed greens or arugula (optional for extra greens)

For the Dressing:

- 3 tbsp olive oil
- 2 tbsp orange juice (freshly squeezed)
- 1 tbsp red wine vinegar
- 1 tsp honey or maple syrup
- 1 tsp Dijon mustard
- Salt and freshly ground black pepper, to taste

Instructions:

1. **Roast the Beets:**
   - Preheat your oven to 400°F (200°C).
   - Toss the beet wedges with a bit of olive oil, salt, and pepper.
   - Spread the beets out on a baking sheet and roast for 35-40 minutes, or until tender and caramelized, tossing halfway through.
2. **Prepare the Dressing:**
   - In a small bowl, whisk together the olive oil, orange juice, red wine vinegar, honey, Dijon mustard, salt, and pepper.
3. **Assemble the Salad:**
   - If using mixed greens or arugula, arrange them on a serving platter or in a large bowl.
   - Add the roasted beets, orange segments, and red onion.
   - Drizzle the dressing over the salad and toss gently to combine.
   - Sprinkle the crumbled goat cheese and chopped nuts over the top.
4. **Serve:**
   - Serve immediately or chill for a bit to allow the flavors to meld.

This salad offers a beautiful balance of sweet and tangy flavors, with a touch of creaminess from the cheese and crunch from the nuts. Enjoy!

Cranberry and Spinach Salad

Ingredients:

For the Salad:

- 4 cups fresh spinach leaves
- 1/2 cup dried cranberries
- 1/4 cup sliced almonds (toasted if desired)
- 1/4 cup crumbled goat cheese or feta cheese
- 1/4 cup thinly sliced red onion (optional)
- 1/2 apple or pear, thinly sliced (optional for added sweetness)

For the Dressing:

- 3 tbsp olive oil
- 2 tbsp balsamic vinegar
- 1 tbsp honey or maple syrup
- 1 tsp Dijon mustard
- 1 clove garlic, minced
- Salt and freshly ground black pepper, to taste

Instructions:

1. **Prepare the Dressing:**
    - In a small bowl, whisk together olive oil, balsamic vinegar, honey, Dijon mustard, minced garlic, salt, and pepper.
2. **Assemble the Salad:**
    - In a large bowl, combine the spinach, dried cranberries, sliced almonds, crumbled cheese, and optional red onion and apple or pear slices.
    - Drizzle the dressing over the salad and toss gently to combine.
3. **Serve:**
    - Serve immediately to keep the spinach crisp.

This salad is a delightful mix of sweet, tangy, and savory flavors with a nice crunch from the almonds. Enjoy!

Lentil and Sweet Potato Salad

Ingredients:

For the Salad:

- 1 cup green or brown lentils (uncooked)
- 2 medium sweet potatoes, peeled and cubed
- 1 tbsp olive oil
- Salt and freshly ground black pepper, to taste
- 1/2 tsp ground cumin (optional)
- 1/2 tsp smoked paprika (optional)
- 1/4 cup chopped fresh parsley or cilantro
- 1/4 cup red onion, finely chopped
- 1/4 cup crumbled feta cheese (optional)
- 1/4 cup chopped walnuts or pecans (toasted if desired)

For the Dressing:

- 3 tbsp olive oil
- 2 tbsp lemon juice
- 1 tbsp red wine vinegar
- 1 tsp Dijon mustard
- 1 tsp honey or maple syrup (optional)
- 1 clove garlic, minced
- Salt and freshly ground black pepper, to taste

Instructions:

1. **Cook the Lentils:**
   - Rinse the lentils under cold water.
   - In a medium saucepan, cover the lentils with water and bring to a boil.
   - Reduce the heat and simmer for about 20-25 minutes, or until the lentils are tender but not mushy. Drain and set aside to cool.
2. **Roast the Sweet Potatoes:**
   - Preheat your oven to 400°F (200°C).
   - Toss the sweet potato cubes with olive oil, salt, pepper, cumin, and smoked paprika (if using).
   - Spread them out in a single layer on a baking sheet.
   - Roast for 25-30 minutes, or until tender and caramelized, tossing halfway through. Let cool.
3. **Prepare the Dressing:**
   - In a small bowl, whisk together olive oil, lemon juice, red wine vinegar, Dijon mustard, honey (if using), minced garlic, salt, and pepper.

4. **Assemble the Salad:**
    - In a large bowl, combine the cooked lentils, roasted sweet potatoes, chopped parsley or cilantro, red onion, and crumbled feta cheese (if using).
    - Pour the dressing over the salad and toss gently to combine.
    - Sprinkle with chopped nuts if desired.
5. **Serve:**
    - Serve warm or at room temperature.

This salad combines the earthiness of lentils with the sweetness of roasted sweet potatoes and the freshness of herbs, making it a wholesome and delicious dish. Enjoy!

www.ingramcontent.com/pod-product-compliance
Lightning Source LLC
LaVergne TN
LVHW081612060526
838201LV00054B/2212